CW01024922

Cali

By United Library

https://campsite.bio/unitedlibrary

Table of Contents

Disclaimer

This biography book is a work of nonfiction based on the public life of a famous person. The author has used publicly available information to create this work. While the author has thoroughly researched the subject and attempted to depict it accurately, it is not meant to be an exhaustive study of the subject. The views expressed in this book are those of the author alone and do not necessarily reflect those of any organization associated with the subject. This book should not be taken as an endorsement, legal advice, or any other form of professional advice. This book was written for entertainment purposes only.

Introduction

Discover the intriguing life of Caligula, the Roman emperor whose reign went from humble beginnings to infamous tyranny. Born into the prestigious Julio-Claudian dynasty, Caligula's early years were marked by tragedy and political strife. Despite initial perceptions of a moderate and noble ruler, Caligula's reign quickly slipped into a maelstrom of extravagance, cruelty, and megalomania.

From ambitious building projects to his proclaimed divinity and alleged plans to appoint his horse as consul, Caligula's rule was marked by scandal and controversy. While some historians dismiss these descriptions as exaggerations or misunderstandings, the image of Caligula as a tyrant persists in historical memory.

Discover the complexities of Caligula's character, his political ambitions and the tumultuous era in which he lived. This biography offers a comprehensive look at one of ancient Rome's best-known figures, exploring the man behind the myths and the lasting impact of his rule.

Explore Caligula's enigmatic life, from his rise to power to his dramatic fall, in this compelling biography.

Caligula

Gaius Julius Caesar Augustus Germanicus (Anzio, August 31, 12 - Rome, January 24, 41), reigned under the name Gaius Caesar and better known by the nickname Caligula, was the third Roman emperor, belonging to the Julio-Claudian dynasty. He reigned for less than four years from 37 to 41, the year of his death.

Historical sources have handed down an image of Caligula as a despot, emphasizing his extravagances, eccentricities, and depravity. He is accused of squandering the wealth accumulated by his predecessor, however much this was also done to fulfill testamentary legacies established by Tiberius and to provide the people with games, money and food. His extravagances, inspired by the autocracy of the Hellenistic Eastern monarchs and contempt for the senatorial class, were not very different from the revenge that Tiberius himself enacted in the last years of his principate.On the other hand, there are aspects that indicate that his initial administration also had positive sides, such as the reduction of the sales tax (*centesima rerum venalium*) and the implementation and renovation of some public works. In his later days he showed signs of mental imbalance, so much so that it is believed he was suffering from a degenerative disease. He was murdered at the age of 28 by soldiers of the Praetorian Guard.

The historiographical sources

Caligula's contemporary historiographical sources that have come down to us are scarce, making him one of the lesser-known Julio-Claudian emperors. His contemporaries were Lucius Anneus Seneca, who recounts some of the Roman emperor's anecdotes, and Philo of Alexandria, who describes the vicissitudes of the Jewish people of that period. Other works contemporary with him were written, which have been lost, and the section of Tacitus' *Annales* dedicated to him is also lost.

So, the most important surviving historiographical sources are Suetonius' *Lives of the Caesars* and Cassius Dion's *Historia romana*, who lived many years after Caligula's death. Both were part of the ruling class opposed to this *princeps*, so much so that the information contained in their works is being reconsidered today in light of their factionalism.

Biography

Family origins

Caligula ("little caligula," the footwear of legionnaires, an affectionate nickname given to him at a young age by his father's soldiers but which he did not want to be used), born as Gaius Julius Caesar Germanicus, was the third son of Agrippina the elder and Germanicus Julius Caesar, a general much loved by the Roman people. His mother was the daughter of Marcus Vipsanius Agrippa (Augustus' close friend) and Julia Major (Augustus' first-born daughter). Her father was the son of Drusus major (brother of Tiberius and son of Livia, wife of Augustus) and Antonia minor (daughter of Mark Antony and Octavia minor, sister of Augustus).

His father Germanicus, moreover, had been adopted by Tiberius at the request of Augustus. This particular family situation (which, through Caesar and his great-grandfather Augustus, made him a descendant of Venus and Aeneas), made Caligula the most likely successor to his great-uncle Tiberius.

His siblings were Nero Caesar, Drusus Caesar, Agrippina Minor (the mother of the future emperor Nero), Drusilla, and Julia Livilla. The first two, older than him, were sent to death by Tiberius; his sister Drusilla, the most beloved, died during his reign, while the other two were exiled by him and returned to Rome only after his death. Caligula also had two other male siblings, Tiberius Caesar (born in 10), Gaius Caesar (born in 11), and a female (born between 13 and 14), but they all died prematurely.

The ancient uncertainty about place of birth

Suetonius narrates that in his time the birthplace of Gaius Caesar was uncertain due to the discordance of sources. In fact, according to Getulicus, whose writings have been lost, however, Caligula was born in Tivoli, while according to Pliny the Elder in *Augusta* Treverorum (Trier). Getulicus is said to have been refuted by Pliny, who accused him of lying out of mere flattery (Tivoli is in fact a city consecrated to Hercules) and of persisting in lying, since his older brother, who died prematurely, also named Gaius, was born in Tivoli. Pliny reports, however, that he spotted a tombstone that read, "In honor of the birth of Agrippina." Suetonius rejects this, arguing that Gaius was already born when his father left for Gaul and that most likely the tombstone referred instead to one of his daughters. Finally, he indicates the city of Anzio as his place of birth, as would appear in official documents.

Youth (12-37)

Born in Anzio on August 31, 12, he was raised in his early years in Rome among the affections of Augustus himself, his great-grandmother Livia, his grandmother Antonia, and his mother Agrippina. In the summer of 14, at the age of almost two, Gaius left with his parents for the Germanic-Gallic front, where he remained until his father had completed his military expeditions to Germany (14 - 16). During these three years, he stayed with his mother near the Rhine (in *Ara Ubiorum*, present-day Cologne), far from the theater of war. Here the first two sisters, Drusilla and Agrippina, were born.

Returning to Rome in 17, after witnessing his father's triumph, he left again with his family for the East. The difficult eastern situation had necessitated a new Roman intervention, and Tiberius in 18 had decided to send his own adopted son, Germanicus, who was granted *imperium proconsulare maius* over all the eastern provinces. The *princeps,* however, had no confidence in Germanicus and decided to place a man of his own proven trust alongside him: the choice fell on Gnaeus Calpurnius Piso, who was appointed governor of the province of Syria. On October 10, 19, his father died after long suffering. Before expiring, Germanicus himself confessed his conviction that he had been poisoned by Piso, and he addressed a final prayer to Agrippina to avenge his death.

Immediately the suspicion arose that it was Piso who had caused his death by poisoning him; rumors also spread that Tiberius himself was involved, as if he were the instigator of Germanicus' murder, having himself personally chosen to send Piso to Syria. The latter was, therefore, recalled to Rome to stand trial and was also accused of having committed numerous other crimes previously. The emperor gave a particularly moderate speech, avoiding taking sides for or against the governor's conviction. Piso, however, could not be charged with the charge of vengeance, which appeared, even to the accusers, impossible to prove; the governor, however, certain that he should be convicted of the other crimes, preferred to commit suicide before the verdict was rendered. The stains on his father's body, the black drool that dripped from his mouth, the heart that remained unscathed by cremation because, as was believed, it seems to have been impregnated with poison, constituted for little Caligula the first signs, horrible and traumatic, of the end of a peaceful childhood, now that he had been confronted with his father's death, intrigues and palace conspiracies.

When Gaius and his mother returned to Rome, Tiberius did not seem happy about their return: the *princeps* and his daughter-in-law suspected each other of poisoning Germanicus. Meanwhile, Sejanus, the prefect of the praetorium, the emperor's friend and confidant, began to engineer Agrippina's demise, leading to rumors that she was to be poisoned. Thus it was that, when during a banquet Tiberius offered her food, she, blatantly rejecting it, provoked the wrath of the emperor, who shortly thereafter accused her of lese majesty in the Senate, along with her son Nero Caesar, who was himself accused of immorality. In 29 Agrippina was exiled to Ventotene, where in 33 she allowed herself to starve to death, while her son Nero, relegated to Ponza, had already died two years earlier, in 31.

Following his mother's exile, Gaius went to live on the Palatine by his paternal great-grandmother, Livia, until her death, when he delivered her eulogy. Forced to move to the abode of his grandmother Antonia, he met several eastern princes who were vassals of Rome and who influenced his politics: the three young Thracian princes, Polemon (to whom he later gave the kingdom of Pontus and Bosporus), Remetalce (to whom he later entrusted half of the ancient kingdom of Thrace) and Cotys (to whom he entrusted that of Armenia Minor). He also met Herod Agrippa (descendant of the kings of Judea of the Herodian dynasty), to whom he remained deeply attached in the years to come by deep friendship, and his cousin Ptolemy of Mauretania (son of Cleopatra Selene, herself the daughter of Cleopatra and Mark Antony and half-sister of his grandmother Antonia). As Suetonius reports, he is said to have deflowered his sister Drusilla during this period and to have been caught in her bed by his grandmother Antonia.

Meanwhile, the imperial court was shrinking in numbers, as Tiberius, fearing that he was at the center of repeated conspiracies, often ordered summary executions. When Sejanus was also suspected of aspiring to the imperial throne, Caligula entered court life more actively. Shortly after the fall of Sejanus (in 31), the question of succession reopened. It was on this occasion that Tiberius, by then retired to Capri since 26, wanted his nephew Caligula to keep him company. Arriving on the island, Gaius received the *toga virilis*, but no additional honor was reserved for him. The boy, during his stay on the island, showed great self-control and seemed to forget all the cruelties that Tiberius had committed against his family. On this occasion the orator Passienus uttered the famous phrase, "There never was a better servant and a worse master."

Suetonius relates that, already during this period, Gaius showed the first signs of his cruel and vicious nature, often and willingly witnessing executions, as well as frequenting taverns and brothels, disguising himself so as not to be recognized. Tiberius, who knew his nephew's vices, tolerated his conduct, and in him sought his personal revenge against the Roman people, who by now hated him, so much so that he uttered the phrase, "Gaius lives for his and everyone's ruin; I raise a viper for the Roman people, a Phaeton for the world."

In 33 Caligula married Junia Claudia, daughter of Marcus Junius Silanus, a prominent figure in the Roman aristocracy. Also in that year Drusus Caesar, the second son of Germanicus, had died after being sentenced to confinement in 30 on charges of conspiring against Tiberius. When his brother died, Gaius replaced him first as augur, then as pontiff.

When Tiberius, in 35, filed his will, having a choice of three possible heirs, he included his nephew Tiberius Gemellus, son of Drusus the younger, and his nephew Gaius, son of Germanicus. This left out the brother of Germanicus himself, Claudius, who was considered wholly unfit for the role of *princeps*, as he was weak in physique and of questionable sanity. The favorite in the succession immediately appeared to be the young Gaius of twenty-five, since Tiberius Gemellus, moreover suspected of actually being the son of Sejanus (for adulterous relations with the wife of Drususus the younger, Claudia Livilla), was ten years younger: two sufficient reasons for not letting him have the principality. At the end of 36 Gaius' wife Junia died in childbirth, but Silanus, Caligula's father-in-law, maintained a deeply filial affection for his son-in-law. Meanwhile, the praetorian prefect Macronius immediately showed sympathy for Gaius, the designated heir, earning his trust by all means, including allowing him to have an adulterous affair with his wife, Ennia Thrasilla.

On March 16, 37, Tiberius' health deteriorated, so that Caligula took to the streets already acclaimed emperor by the people. Tiberius, however, soon afterwards recovered once more, causing havoc among those who had prematurely acclaimed the new emperor; the prefect Macrone, however, maintaining the necessary lucidity, ordered that Tiberius be smothered in blankets. The old emperor, weak and unable to react, expired at the age of seventy-seven. According to Suetonius, it was Caligula himself who killed Tiberius by either administering poison or suffocating him on his deathbed. According to Tiberius' contemporaries, however, the Prince died of natural causes.

Ascent to the Throne (37)

When Tiberius died, the designated heirs were Caligula and Tiberius Gemellus. The latter, however, had not yet reached adulthood (age 15), while Gaius was the most beloved of the Roman people. Soldiers and provincials remembered him when, while still a child, he had accompanied his father Germanicus on military campaigns, and the Roman plebs acclaimed him as the only son of the beloved general.

Caligula returned to Rome following Tiberius' funeral procession and, upon entering the city, delivered his eulogy. Immediately afterwards he left for the islands of Ventotene and Ponza to bring back to Rome the ashes of his mother and brother Nero. He took them reverently and placed them in urns himself; then he sailed to Ostia and proceeded to Rome where he placed them in the mausoleum of Augustus. The crowd as he passed acclaimed him, calling him "our star" and "our child." The Senate then, under pressure from the people, annulled Tiberius' will, on the grounds that the emperor before his death had lost his mind, and proclaimed Caligula the new *princeps.* This was on March 18, 37.

The Parthian king, Artabanus II, who had always declared his hatred of Tiberius, paid tribute to the new *princeps* by offering him an alliance between the two peoples. In the period that followed the beginning of his principate, free feasts and banquets were often organized for the entire citizenry of Rome (*congiaria*): Suetonius adds that in the three months following Caligula's proclamation, more than 160,000 animals were sacrificed, while Philo records that during the first seven months of his reign all the citizens were constantly celebrating.

CÆSONIA wife of CALIGULA.

The principality (37-41)

First Acts (37)

To please the people, one of his first official acts was to grant amnesty to the condemned, those exiled by Tiberius, and all those who were defendants in a trial. To appease the witnesses in the trial of his mother and brothers, he had all the trial files brought into the Forum and burned them. He declared that sexual perverts, inventors of monstrous couplings, should be expelled from the Urbe and sent into exile; he allowed the once-banned writings of Titus Labienus, Cassius Severus, and Cremutius Chordus (which denounced the senatorial class in many cases) to be researched, disseminated, and read. He implemented other reforms to improve the conditions of the republic, increase the freedom of citizens, and fight corruption.

He organized public banquets and extended the *Saturnalia* holiday by one day. He often organized free shows and games to make himself well-liked by the population. He also devised a new kind of spectacle: between Baia and Pozzuoli he had a bridge built, more than two and a half kilometers long, consisting of two rows of ships anchored and covered with earth, in the likeness of the Appian Way. Because of the huge number of ships used, food was scarce throughout Rome for a few days, as there were insufficient means of supplying the city, which along the Tiber led foodstuffs from the provinces to the port of Ostia and from there to the Urbe. Not only in the Urbe did he organize these kinds of events, but also in Sicily (particularly in Syracuse) and Gaul (in *Lugdunum*).

He completed some public works begun by his predecessor, such as the Temple of Augustus, as well as renovating others such as the Theatre of Pompey. He began construction of the Aqueduct Claudius (finished by his successor and from which he took his name), the Aqueduct Anio novus, and a new amphitheater at the site of elections (which was abandoned upon his death, however). He reconstructed many buildings and temples in Syracuse. He planned the renovation of the palace of Polycrates in Samos, the Temple of Apollo in Miletus, the foundation of a city in the Alps, and the cutting of the Isthmus of Corinth. He had the obelisk that stood in the forum at Heliopolis brought to Rome and placed it in the center of a circus that he began to build but was completed by Nero and named after him. Finally, he renovated the ports of Reggio Calabria and Sicily in order to increase the import of grain from Egypt.

Provincial administration

In 37, the first year of his reign, Caligula faced a natural disaster in Antioch of Syria: an earthquake occurred on April 9 that destroyed the city. The emperor, using money left to him from the principate of Tiberius, immediately arranged to begin reconstruction work and sent a legate, a certain Salvianus, and two senators, Lurius Varius and Pontius, to oversee and verify it. The three also made many offerings to the city, building baths and a Trinymphon for weddings.

In 38 Caligula sent one of his friends, Herod Agrippa, against the prefect of Egypt, Aulus Avilius Flaccus, an alleged conspirator to the imperial purple who had ties to Egyptian separatists. The Greek population of Alexandria frowned upon Agrippa, as he was a Jewish king. Flaccus then tried to appease both the emperor and the Greeks by having his statues erected in synagogues. It was all in vain, for revolt broke out in the city anyway; Flaccus was therefore removed from office and shortly afterward executed.

In 40 a new revolt broke out in Alexandria, Egypt, between Greeks and Jews: the latter were accused of impiety against the emperor because they had destroyed his statues in places of worship. Caligula's reaction was the decision taken to have a colossal statue of him erected inside the temple in Jerusalem itself, which clashed with Jewish monotheistic belief. The governor of

Syria, Publius Petronius, was given orders to intervene with the army, but Agrippa was able to convince him that this was not necessary, and the emperor agreed not to use force against the Jewish people.

Economic and financial administration

When Tiberius died, there were as many as 2 700 000 000 sesterces in the coffers of the Roman *fiscus,* which Caligula managed to squander in less than a year. This enormous fund that he inherited from his predecessor was squandered in late 38 and early 39. Numerous were in fact the handouts distributed to the people of Rome (*congiaria*), to the provincial armies and the praetorian guard (to whom he conferred a donation double that promised by Tiberius, amounting to 2 000 sesterces each), to the vassal kingdoms of Rome (Antiochus IV of Commagene alone received 100 000 000 sesterces), as well as expenditures for personal use and that of the imperial court.

Suetonius adds that he had very expensive baths built, consisting of huge tubs with alternating hot and cold waters. He had pearls dissolved in vinegar and food sprinkled with powdered gold served, claiming that he had to be either a frugal man or a Caesar. He appropriated a sum that was daily thrown from the Basilica Julia onto the crowd below. He built ships of disproportionate size, with ten orders of oars, decorated with precious gems and gaudy colors, on which were placed baths, dining rooms, porticoes and vine plantations. He saw to it that his architects raised immense dams, excavated mountains and produced silting up of valleys in a very short time.

In this early period, he also disclosed all accounts of public funds, as Augustus had also done in the past but not Tiberius, at least since he had moved away from Rome. He helped soldiers put out a fire and gave assistance to those who had damage due to natural events, as well as abolishing the 1 percent tax on goods sold at auction (*centesima rerum venalium*).

When he ran out of state funds he began to accumulate money through swindling and cheating. It is said that he organized compulsory auctions of all kinds; altered wills for the most disparate reasons, appointing himself heir to strangers; refused to recognize citizenship to a great many people, declaring that the deeds before Tiberius' principate were too old; he indicted those whose wealth had grown from one census to the next, prosecuting them and obtaining huge sums of money in a very short time; he increased taxes out of all proportion and created totally new ones, such as those on food, lawsuits, prostitution, marriages, and gambling. Finally, the new laws were not made completely public in such a way that, ignorant of their existence, they were violated, thus generating heavy fines that fed the imperial coffers.

Judicial administration and orders

In general, Caligula's judicial policy can be divided into two periods: the first, very liberal and pro-people, in which he also sought the favor of the senatorial order; the second, in which the *princeps* did everything to increase his own power, in a kind of monarchical absolutism, which he exploited to accumulate wealth and to dispose of the fate of Roman citizens as he pleased.

Since the equestrian order was shrinking in numbers, he summoned from all over the empire, even outside Italy, the most important men by lineage and wealth and enrolled them in the order; to indulge their expectation of becoming senators, he allowed some of them to wear senatorial robes even before they had taken office in those magistracies that gave access to the Senate. He sought to restore, at least formally, the powers of the popular assemblies by allowing the plebs to convene rallies again.

CALIGVLA

Nec Deus es, nec homo, Cai. sub principe magistrum es,
Si qua Dicarchæas utnæsse est nauibus artes
Eubœa laus parta uiga. at spolia ampla reportat

Dictæne Oceani lec fis in litore conchis.
Veq tibi fultu plausisti sirucus in auro,
Sic quoq; læta tuo te sanguine Roma uidit est

Foreign Policy

West

The fact that Caligula belonged to a family of prominent military commanders who had earned glory and honor through feats of war may have aroused in him a desire to emulate their exploits. If Drusus Major, his paternal grandfather, and Germanicus, his father, had concentrated in Germany, he, in order to surpass their exploits, believed that he had to not only conquer permanently the territories between the Danube and the Rhine, but also cross the ocean and land in Britain. To this end, he first created two new legions, the *XV Primigenia* and the *XXII Primigenia*.

Leaving Rome in early September 39, he led his army along the Rhine, amassing numerous legions there, together with their auxiliary units and a large amount of provisions. In October, after reviewing the troops, he had Gnaeus Cornelius Lentulus Getulicus, who had been the governor of Upper Germania for ten years, killed because he envied his excellent relationship with his troops.

His enterprise proved almost entirely futile, except that Adminius, son of Cunobelinus king of the Britons, driven out by his father, came to the emperor's camp and made an act of submission. Caligula remained on the Rhine without completing any military operations, however, and reproached the senators for living among luxuries while he risked his life in battle. He then decided to move troops toward the Ocean, taking with him numerous war machines. He ordered his men to take off their helmets and collect shells on the beach, as if they were the spoils of a battle won against the sea. He finally had a great tower built there in memory of his victorious exploits and bestowed rewards on his soldiers.

Modern historians have advanced some theories to explain these kinds of actions: the journey to the Channel is interpreted as an exercise, a scouting mission or to accept the surrender of the British leader Adminio. Instead, the "shells" (Latin *conchae*) mentioned by Suetonius may represent a metaphor for female genitalia, as the troops were probably allowed to frequent brothels in the area; or of Briton boats, which the soldiers may have captured during the short expedition.

East

In the East, Caligula installed as client kings the three young Thracian princes he had had the opportunity to associate with in his youth at his grandmother Antonia's house: to Polemon II the kingdom of Pontus and the Bosporus (in 38), to Remetalce III half of the ancient kingdom of Thrace, and to Cotys IX Armenia Minor. The emperor did not follow an identical political line with the eastern allied kingdoms: he relied heavily on the sympathy and personal trust that each individual ruler was able to convey to him. He deposed and exiled Mithridates, king of Armenia; appointed Antiochus king of Commagene, a region reduced to a province in 17, to whom he gave 100 million sesterces; elected as governor of the territories of Batanea and Traconitide his childhood friend, Herod Agrippa, later also giving him the kingdom of Judea after exiling his uncle Herod Antipas (in 39), who was accused of wanting to seize Agrippa's territories and of plotting a conspiracy against the emperor, as well as northwestern Palestine, which since the death of Herod Philip II (34) had been under the direct control of Rome.

African front

Mauretania had long been a client kingdom loyal to Rome, ruled by Ptolemy of Mauretania, a descendant of Antony and Cleopatra and a second cousin of the prince. In 40 Caligula invited Ptolemy to Rome, and "when he learned that he was rich," he sent him to his death. After the killing of the king of Mauritania a revolt broke out led by one of his freedmen, Edemone, who had been administering royal affairs since 37, and which ended thanks to the Roman military intervention of Marcus Licinius Crassus Frugi (41). Mauretania was then annexed and later divided into two provinces, Mauretania Tingitana and Mauretania Cesariensis, separated by the

Mulucha (now Muluia) River. While Pliny claims that the division was effected by Caligula, Cassius Dione on the contrary states that it was only following the revolt of 42, which was smothered in blood by Roman troops placed under the command of Gaius Suetonius Paulinus and Gnaeus Osidius Geta, that the split into two independent provinces was effected; this confusion may have been generated by the fact that it was Caligula who made the decision to divide the province, but that its implementation was postponed because of the subsequent rebellion. The first equestrian governor of the two provinces was a certain Marcus Phadius Celerus Flavianus Maximus (44).

The details of the conquest of Mauritania are unclear although Cassius Dione had devoted an entire chapter to it, unfortunately lost. The annexation operated by Caligula seems to have had a strictly personal motive, namely the fear and jealousy of the *princeps'* cousin Ptolemy. The expansion would thus not have been driven, at least initially, by economic or strategic-military needs. However, the Tacfarinas rebellion had shown how weak Proconsular Africa was along its western borders and how important the client kings of Mauretania were in providing their protection to the province, and it is therefore possible that the annexation operated by Caligula represented a strategic response to potential future threats.

Sickness (October of 37)

From a young age Caligula was prone to sudden fainting spells:

In October 37, the emperor was stricken with a serious illness, news that deeply disturbed the Roman people, who made vows for the salvation of their *princeps*; Suetonius and Cassius Dione report the case of a knight, Atanius Secundus, who promised to fight in the arena as a gladiator in the event of his recovery: he kept his promise, fighting, winning the fight and saving his life. In contrast, a commoner who made an identical promise, following Gaius' recovery, claimed to dissolve the vow, but was arrested and died after being thrown from the Servian walls.

Caligula recovered from his illness, although from this time on there was a marked deterioration in his moral conduct. On the illness and causes historians do not agree, but all regard this event as the watershed between his first period of rule and the next, characterized by insane conduct. Philo of Alexandria observes:

For Philo, God used Caligula, transforming him after his illness from an excellent prince and fortunate heir to Tiberius into a crazed executioner destined to carry out divine vengeance against the Jews and Romans, the same vengeance that would later punish his persecutor, eventually freeing the Israelites themselves.

The illness was attributed to the excesses committed early in the principate; in particular Juvenal and Suetonius point to the use of an aphrodisiac (*poculum amatorium*) offered to him by his wife Milonia Cesonia as the cause of Caligula's madness. Actual mental disorders (schizophrenia, bipolar disorder, or others), diseases such as epilepsy, hyperthyroidism (e.g., Hashimoto's thyroiditis), herpetic encephalitis, neurolue, and saturnism have been hypothesized by modern scholars as causes of the mood swings, hallucinations, insomnia, and paranoia from which the emperor suffered.

Decline (38-41)

It was during this period that Gaius understood what risks he was facing, as the office of emperor was coveted by many. Although he fully recovered from his illness, his way of ruling changed profoundly. Ancient sources described him as "mad" endowed with a "bloodthirsty madness."

His brief principate was characterized, in fact, by repeated massacres of opponents, and by acts of government aimed at humiliating the senatorial class and the entire Roman nobility. Famous is the episode of his beloved horse, *Incitatus*, whom, according to a tradition reported by Suetonius and Cassius Dione, Caligula vowed to appoint consul, an extreme purpose of taunting the senators to which, however, he did not follow up in his few years of reign. His despotic behavior resulted in numerous conspiracies, all foiled except the last.

Caligula, soon after his illness, assumed autocratic and provocative attitudes. He was accused, in fact, of lying with the wives of prominent members of the Roman aristocracy and bragging about it; of killing for sheer amusement; of deliberately squandering state property; and of ordering the erection of a colossal statue in the Temple of Jerusalem, defying the religious customs of the

Jews. He, on the other hand, made himself extremely popular with lavish handouts to the plebs and expensive circus games, but the people also turned against him when he raised taxes again.

If the emperors before him had chosen, at least in the western part of the empire, to maintain ties with republican traditions, he veered noticeably eastward: not only did he plan to move the imperial capital to Alexandria, Egypt (as his great-grandfather Mark Antony wanted), but also to establish a form of absolute monarchy, at that time still unknown in Italy but in fact put in place by Domitian, Commodus, and all Roman emperors from the third century onward. He adopted, therefore, a policy of becoming a ruler to whom divine honors were rendered on the model of Eastern monarchies, exacerbating the well-known process of deifying deceased emperors.

His pro-Hellenist leanings eventually caused him to plan a long trip to Alexandria, Asia Minor and Syria.

Caligula prince and goddess

When a number of foreign rulers came to Rome to pay homage to the emperor and to discuss their noble family origins, Caligula cried out, "Let there be one leader, one king," and was on the verge of restoring the monarchy on the spot. In 40 Caligula began a highly controversial policy of juxtaposing the title of prince with the role of deity: in fact, he began appearing in public dressed as gods and demigods of the Roman pantheon, such as Hercules, Venus, and Apollo. He began referring to himself as a god, calling himself *Jupiter* in public ceremonies.

Obsessed with the idea of kingship, he saw it personified in Jupiter, the king of all gods, whose epithets Caligula took up in the *cognomina*: *Optimus Maximus Caesar*. With Capitoline Jupiter the emperor maintained a confidential relationship, almost one of brotherhood and complicity. Suetonius reports:

This, which may appear to be bizarre behavior, was actually part of Roman religious customs, as other ancient sources report about Scipio Africanus who habitually had mystical dialogues with Capitoline Jupiter. Caligula's blasphemous phrase addressed to Jupiter ("either you eliminate me or I you"), Cassius Dione relates, should be referred to the emperor's annoyance with Jupiter Thundering, whose thunder and lightning, of which he was moreover afraid, had prevented him from quietly attending the pantomime performances, and in response to and in opposition to the god

A sacred place prepared for the emperor's worship was inaugurated in Miletus, in the province of Asia, and two other temples were erected in Rome. The temple of Castor and Pollux was attached by Caligula to the imperial palace on the Palatine and was dedicated to the *princeps*. Suetonius tells how the prince went so far as to extend part of the palace to the Forum and turned the temple of Castor and Pollux into his own vestibule, often sitting between the statues of the two divine brothers so as to offer himself for the adoration of passers-by. He also had the heads of several statues of gods removed and replaced with his own. It was said that he wanted to be worshipped as *Neos Helios*, the "New Sun"; in fact, he was depicted as this deity on Egyptian coins.

Caligula's religious policy was very different from that of the other Roman emperors; in fact, emperors in life were worshipped as gods only in the East, while in Rome they were worshipped as gods only after death. Caligula began to have the citizens of Rome, including senators, worship him as a living god.

Personal life

Honors to his family

In honor of his mother Agrippina he had new circus games instituted, during which a statue of the woman was carried in procession on a par with the gods. In memory of his father, he changed the name of the month of September to *Germanicus*, proclaimed an annual day of sacrifices in honor of his brothers. and by senate-consultation had his grandmother Antonia bestowed all the honors Livia Augusta had formerly enjoyed. He took his uncle Claudius as a colleague during his first consulship, adopted Tiberius Gemellus on the day he reached adulthood, and named him *Princeps Iuventutis*. He had a formula included in every oath to remember his sisters, "I shall not cherish myself and my children more than Gaius Caesar and his sisters," and likewise in relations between consuls, "For the prosperity and fortune of Gaius and his sisters." It was also decreed that the day on which he had assumed power should be called *Parilia* (April 21, the date of Rome's founding), as if the state had been born a second time.

Relationships with family members

While Caligula at the beginning of his reign honored his family members, over time his relationship with them deteriorated. Suetonius recounts that he preferred to conceal that he was Agrippa's grandson, as he was attributed humble origins, claiming instead that his mother was born of incest between Julia the Elder and Augustus himself, thus bringing the image of the first Roman emperor into disrepute. He often mocked his great-grandmother Livia Drusilla, calling her an "Ulysses in skirts" and reproaching her that her grandfather, Alfidius Lurcone, was a mere decurion of *Fundi*. The only ancestor of his he had respect for was Mark Antony: Cassius Dione tells us that when the two incumbent consuls celebrated Augustus' victory over Antony, Caligula removed them from office. This appreciation of Antony was probably due to the tales of his grandmother Antonia, daughter of the triumvir, from whom he also took the common passion for Hellenism.

He preferred to receive his grandmother Antonia not in private but in the presence of the praetorian prefect Macrone; later, according to some sources, he had her killed by poisoning her. Suetonius reports that Antonia died of an illness caused by hostile treatment by Caligula, although he adds that there were rumors that claimed she was made to poison by her nephew, while according to Dion Cassius Caligula made her commit suicide because she reproached him. He also had his cousin Tiberius Gemellus killed by falsely accusing him of making an attempt on her life, thus ridding himself of this inconvenient rival. He also forced his father-in-law Marcus Junius Silanus to commit suicide, also accusing him of making an attempt on his life. In the latter case it seems that some testimonies were "bought", including that of Senator Julius Grecinus, who, however, eventually refused to confess to perjury and was therefore put to death. As for Uncle Claudius, he kept him alive only to make him his laughingstock and object of amusement.

With the three sisters he had a very close, if complicated, relationship, especially with Drusilla. He was in fact jealous of her husband, Lucius Cassius Longinus, forcing them to divorce; he treated her as if she were his wife and when she fell ill he named her heir to the imperial throne. He entertained incestuous relations with all three and did not hide it publicly.

When Drusilla died, he suspended all kinds of activities and held public funerals for her, deifying her on Sept. 23, 38, with a senate consulate. As a result of this bereavement, the *princeps* was particularly grieved to the extent that her health deteriorated. Regarding the other two sisters, however, he did not have the same complicity that he did with Drusilla. At the trial of Marcus Aemilius Lepidus, to whom he had previously promised succession, he convicted them of adultery and sent them into exile on the Ponzian Islands.

Weddings

After the death of his first wife around 36, Caligula began an intimate relationship with Ennia Thrasilla, wife of the loyal prefect of the Praetorium Quintus Nevius Sutorius Macronius. In late 37, during the wedding feast of Gaius Calpurnius Piso and Livia Orestilla, he ordered her husband to repudiate his bride so that he could remarry her the same day. It happened, however, that after a few days he repudiated her in turn, sending her into exile two months later so that she would not be allowed to remarry Piso.

The following year (in 38), he married Lollia Paulina, wife of the consul and provincial governor Publius Memmius Regulus. Caligula, who had heard that his grandmother Aurelia had been a beautiful woman in her youth, summoned Pauline from the province, divorced her from her husband, and remarried her. He soon divorced her as well, declaring that she was barren and sent her back, ordering her, however, not to have carnal relations with anyone else.

Also in 38, when Macron was appointed prefect of Egypt, Ennia was also forced to leave along with her husband and children. Just before setting sail for his new destination, Caligula, evidently grieving over feeling abandoned by his mistress, ordered her, her husband, and their children to commit suicide.

Finally, in 39, he began a relationship with Milonia Cesonia, who became his concubine; after divorcing Pauline, he married her since she was pregnant. Milonia Cesonia was neither young nor beautiful, but Caligula felt a real passion for her. After a month of marriage a child was born, who was given the name Julia Drusilla, in memory of her deceased sister and deified upon her death.

Death and Succession (41)

Suetonius reports in the *Life of Gaius* that many events had foretold Caligula's death: some thunderbolts struck the Capitol of Capua and the Temple of Apollo Palatine in Rome on the Ides of March, the same day as Caesar's assassination, and the astrologer Sulla had also predicted to him that he was close to death. The Fortune deities of Anzio warned him about the existence of a certain Cassius who was ready to assassinate him; he then, believing it to be the proconsul of Asia Cassius Longinus, had him recalled and assassinated (according to Suetonius' account) or perhaps only imprisoned (according to what Cassius Dione handed down). Caligula forgot, however, that there was another Cassius, the tribune of the praetorian guard Cassius Cherea, who actually had an active part in his murder.

The assassination of the emperor was organized mainly by three people, including the tribune Cassius Cherea, although many knights, senators, and military men knew about it, as did the powerful imperial adviser Callistus and the prefect of the praetorium. Cherea, in particular, had political reasons and personal motives for killing his *princeps*: it is said that Caligula often sneered at him because of the high-pitched tones of his voice, claiming that he was effeminate and calling him "queer" (*gunnis*), making obscene gestures behind his back or forcing him to use watchwords such as "Priapus," "Love," or "Venus" for his service. Other prominent conspirators were Lucius Annius Vinicianus, who joined the conspiracy to avenge his friend Lepidus, and Senator Marcus Cluvius Rufus.

On January 24, 41, during the annual celebration of the *ludi palatini*, a group of praetorians, led by the two tribunes Cherea and Cornelius Sabinus, put their plan to assassinate the *princeps into action.* The occasion was favorable, as the conspirators would be able to mingle with the spectators who had flocked to the mobile theater traditionally set up in front of the imperial palace. Caligula arrived at the theater, sat down and began to watch the performance. When around the seventh hour, or perhaps the ninth, depending on the sources, he decided to leave, and as he walked through a cryptoporticus that connected the theater to the palace, he stopped to converse with a group of Asian actors who were to perform shortly. It was at this point that the prince finally met his dreaded fate. At the first tumult, litter bearers, armed with sticks, rushed to his aid, then the Germans of his guard, who killed some of his assassins and also some senators unconnected with the crime. During the confrontation Caligula was stabbed to death. A few hours later his wife Milonia Cesonia also lost her life, stabbed by a centurion specially sent by Cherea, and his young daughter, Julia Drusilla, who was thrown against a wall. According to Suetonius, the prince was hit by more than thirty stab wounds. His corpse was taken to the *Horti Lamiani*, half-burned and hastily covered with earth; when the sisters returned from exile, they dug up their brother's body and laid his ashes in the Mausoleum of Augustus.

When the news spread that Caligula had died, no one dared to celebrate, as most believed that the emperor had put the rumor out there to see who he could trust. When this communication was confirmed, however, as the conspirators had not named any other emperor, the Senate met and declared that they wanted to restore the Republic, effectively erasing the rule of the previous *principes* starting with Augustus. Cherea tried to convince the army to support the conscript fathers, but to no avail. Eventually the senators realized that they had to appoint a new successor, whom Lucius Annius Vinicianus, a prominent senator and conspirator, pointed to Marcus Vinicius, his relative and husband of Julia Livilla.

When Caligula died, there were few remaining members of the imperial family still alive. Among them was the 50-year-old Claudius, who, upon learning of the death of his nephew Gaius, ran to hide in his rooms; tracked down by a praetorian while hiding behind a tent, he was led to their camp to be acclaimed emperor while the Senate was busy between the Forum and Capitol. Claudius was invited to appear before the people, but first he decided to buy the loyalty of the praetorian guard by promising the sum of fifteen thousand sesterces for each praetorian.

Thus it was that Claudius was elevated to the imperial purple and became the fourth emperor of Rome. The new *princeps* then vetoed what the Senate had just resolved: to condemn Caligula to *damnatio memoriae*. Then, at the invitation of the Roman people, he had all the conspirators, including Cassius Cherea, imprisoned and sentenced to death.

Burial place

As mentioned, according to Suetonius' account, Caligula was buried first quickly in the *Horti Lamiani* and then permanently in the Mausoleum of Augustus, where most members of the Julio-Claudian dynasty were interred. There, in 410, during the sack of Rome by the Visigoths of Alaric I, the funerary urn containing his ashes was taken from the structure and its contents dispersed, as was the case on that occasion for all the urns of the dynasty. However, according to modern historiography, it is unlikely that Caligula's ashes had been moved from the *Horti Lamiani* and admitted inside the Mausoleum, even given the policy of *damnatio memoriae* against him promoted by Claudius; nevertheless, it is impossible to rule out this hypothesis given the scarcity of sources and findings on the matter.

A further hypothesis, considered unlikely by the academic community, would have it that Caligula was buried in Nemi, the location where the emperor resided. In fact, on January 17, 2011, police in Nemi announced that they had discovered a possible burial place for the emperor Caligula, after arresting a thief trying to take away a statue attributed to this very emperor. However, the news, reported mainly in the British press, was greeted with great skepticism by Cambridge University historian Mary Beard, who considered such a hypothesis unfounded. According to *National Geographic,* the fact would not prove that Nemi was Caligula's burial place since the object of the theft, the large, piecemeal statue depicting Caligula seated on a throne, may once have been located in the hold of Nemi's ships sunk in the lake of the same name.

Imperial coinage of the period

The coinage of the Julio-Claudians refers to all the coins issued by Rome during the principality of the five emperors of the Julio-Claudian dynasty-Augustus, Tiberius, Caligula, Claudius, and Nero (27 BCE to 68).

Historical context

The *Julio-Claudii* represent the dynasty, so called, from the *nomen* (the family name) of the first two emperors: Gaius Julius Caesar Octavian (the Emperor Augustus), adopted by Caesar and therefore a member of the Julian family (*gens* Iulia) and Tiberius Claudius Nero (the Emperor Tiberius first-bed son of Livia, Augustus' wife), who belonged by birth to the Claudia family (*gens* Claudia).

Tiberius

A descendant of the *gens Claudia*, at birth he was given the name Tiberius Claudius *Nero (Tiberius Claudius Nero)*. He was adopted by Augustus in A.D. 4, and his name changed to Tiberius Julius Caesar (*Tiberius Iulius Caesar*); upon the death of his adoptive father (Aug. 19, 14), he was given the name Tiberius Julius Caesar *Augustus* *(Tiberius Iulius Caesar Augustus)* and was able to officially succeed him as *princeps*, although he had been associated in the government of the empire since the year 12.

In his youth Tiberius distinguished himself for his military talent by brilliantly leading numerous campaigns along the northern borders of the Empire (in Germania and Illyricum). After a period of voluntary exile on the island of Rhodes, he returned to Rome in 4 and led further expeditions to Illyricum and Germany, where he remedied the aftermath of the Battle of Teutoburg. Having ascended the throne, he made some important reforms in the economic and political spheres, and ended the policy of military expansion, limiting himself to keeping the borders secure thanks in part to the work of his nephew Germanicus. After the latter's death, Tiberius increasingly favored the rise of the prefect of the praetorium Sejanus, moving away from Rome and retiring to the island of Capri. When the prefect showed he wanted to seize absolute power, Tiberius had him dismissed and killed, but he still avoided returning to the capital.

And while Tiberius was harshly criticized by ancient historians such as Tacitus and Suetonius, his figure has been reevaluated by modern historiography as that of a skillful and careful politician.

Main themes

Imperial family and succession

From the very beginning of his principate, Tiberius had to live with the incredible prestige that Germanicus, the son of his brother, Drusus the Elder, whom he himself had adopted by order of Augustus, was acquiring among all the people of Rome.

By the time the latter had completed his campaigns on the northern front, where he had earned the esteem of his associates and legionnaires by succeeding in recovering two of the three *Legionary Eagles* lost at the Battle of Teutoburg, his popularity was such that he could, if he wished, seize power by ousting his adoptive father, who in some contexts was already frowned upon since his rise to the principate had been marked by the death of all the other relatives whom Augustus had named as heirs.

Resentment therefore prompted Tiberius to give his adopted son a special assignment in the East, so as to further distance him from Rome; the Senate accordingly decided to confer on the young man the *imperium proconsulare maius* over all the eastern provinces, accompanied by Gnaeus Calpurnius Piso, who had been a colleague in Tiberius' own consulship in 7 B.C., sour and inflexible. Germanicus, therefore, left in 18 for the East together with Piso, who was appointed governor of the province of Syria.

Germanicus, who had returned to Syria in 19 after sojourning in Egypt during the winter, came into open conflict with Piso, who had nullified all the measures Tiberius' young stepson had taken; Piso, in response, decided to leave the province and return to Rome. Shortly after Piso's departure, Germanicus fell ill in Antioch and died on October 10 after long suffering; before expiring, Germanicus himself confessed his conviction that he had been poisoned by Piso, and he addressed a final prayer to Agrippina to avenge his death. Tiberius, however, avoided publicly expressing his feelings, and did not even participate in the ceremony in which Germanicus' ashes were placed in Augustus' mausoleum. In fact, Germanicus may have died a natural death, but growing popularity greatly emphasized the event, which, however, is also exaggerated by the historian Tacitus.

Immediately, however, the suspicion arose, fueled by the words spoken by the dying Germanicus, that it was Piso who had caused his death by poisoning him. Thus, rumors also spread of Tiberius' own involvement, as if he were the instigator of Germanicus' murder, having himself personally chosen to send Piso to Syria:

Germanicus' death opened the way for succession to Tiberius' only natural son, Drusus, who had, up to that point, accepted a secondary role to his cousin Germanicus. He was only a year younger than the deceased, but equally able, as is evident from the way he dealt with the revolt in Pannonia. Meanwhile, Lucius Aelius Sejanus, appointed prefect of the Praetorium along with his father in 16, soon succeeded in winning Tiberius' trust. Alongside Drusus, therefore, who was favored for the succession, came also the figure of Sejanus, who acquired a great influence on Tiberius's work: the prefect of the Praetorium, in fact, who showed in character a reserve quite similar to that of the emperor, was instead animated by a strong desire for power, and aspired himself to become Tiberius's successor.

A situation of open rivalry then arose between Drusus and Sejanus; the prefect then began to ponder the possibility of assassinating Drusus and the other possible successors of Tiberius, seduced Drusus's own wife, Claudia Livilla, and engaged in an affair with her. A short time later, in 23, Drusus himself died of poisoning; public opinion came to suspect, though without any foundation, that it might have been Tiberius who ordered the assassination of Drusus, but it appeared more likely that Claudia Livilla had been involved. Eight years later, Tiberius learned that it was his own daughter-in-law Livilla who had killed his son, along with his most trusted adviser, Sejanus.

Sejanus, having eliminated the last direct descendant of Tiberius, now considered himself the only candidate for succession. He began, therefore, to aspire to the conferment of the *tribunicia potestas*, which would formally sanction his subsequent appointment as emperor, making his person sacred and inviolable, and obtained, meanwhile, in 31 the consulship along with Tiberius himself. At the same time, however, the widow of Drusus major, Antonia minor, making herself the spokeswoman for the sentiments of a large part of the senatorial class, communicated in a letter to Tiberius all the intrigues and bloody deeds for which Sejanus, who was hatching a conspiracy against the emperor himself, was responsible; Tiberius, alerted decided then to dismiss the powerful prefect, and organized a skillful maneuver with the help of the prefect of Urbe Macrone.

Eventually, the emperor accused the prefect of treason and ordered his dismissal and arrest. Sejanus, stunned by the unexpected volte-face was immediately led away in chains by the *vigiles* and shortly thereafter summarily tried by the Senate assembled in the temple of Concord: he was sentenced to death and *damnatio memoriae*:

Triumphs in Germany and Illyricum

Tiberius, after completing operations in *Germania Magna* and *Illyricum*, celebrated a well-deserved triumph in Rome in October 12, on which occasion he prostrated himself publicly before Augustus, and obtained in 13 the renewal of *tribunicia potestas* and *imperium proconsulare maius*, titles that effectively completed his succession, elevating him to the effective rank of co-regent, along with Augustus himself: he could, therefore, administer the provinces, command the armies, and fully exercise executive power. From the moment of his adoption, however, Tiberius had already begun to take an active part in the government of the state, assisting his stepfather in enacting laws and in administration.

Caligula

The third emperor of the Julio-Claudian dynasty was Caligula, about whom the surviving historical sources have made him notorious for his extravagance, eccentricity and depravity, handing down an image of a despot. The paucity of sources, however, makes Caligula the least known of all the emperors of the dynasty.

By the time Tiberius died, many of the people who might have succeeded him had been killed. The most logical successor (also chosen by Tiberius) was Gaius (better known as Caligula, for his habit of wearing special sandals called *caligae*), his great-grandson and son of the heir to the throne, Germanicus, who died prematurely in 19.

Caligula began his reign by ending the persecutions and burning his uncle's archives. Unfortunately, however, he soon fell ill: later historians, probably partially altering the truth, report a series of his senseless acts that allegedly took place beginning in late 37. It appears, for example, that he ordered his soldiers to invade Britannia, but changed his mind at the last minute, sending them instead to collect shells on the seashore. He was, moreover, accused of having incestuous relations with his own sisters. Also famous is his alleged decision to appoint one of his horses as senator. His order to erect a statue of him in the temple in Jerusalem, although it was standard practice in the eastern provinces (where worship reserved for the ruler functioned as an institutional glue), sparked opposition from the Jews.

In 41, Caligula fell victim to a conspiracy, assassinated by Praetorian commander Cassius Cherea. The only remaining member of the imperial family was another nephew of Tiberius: Tiberius Claudius Drusus Nero Germanicus, better known as Claudius.

Imperial family

Caligula was the third son of Agrippina Major and Germanicus, a general much loved by the Roman people. His father was the son of Drusus Major (brother of Tiberius and son of Livia, wife of Augustus) and Antonia Minor (daughter of Mark Antony and Octavia, sister of Augustus). His mother was the daughter of Marcus Vipsanius Agrippa (Augustus' friend) and Julia (Augustus' first-born daughter). In addition, her father Germanicus had been adopted by Tiberius, who had been adopted by Augustus, who in turn had been adopted by Julius Caesar. He had, in addition, eight including, Nero Caesar, Drusus, Agrippina Minor, Julia Drusilla, and Julia Livilla.

Finally, he had four wives-Junia Claudilla, Livia Orestilla, Lollia Paolina, formerly married to Publius Memmius Regulus, and Milonia Caesonia, by whom he had a daughter whom he named Julia Drusilla in honor of his beloved sister who died of illness, Livia Drusilla.

Claudio

Born Tiberius Claudius Drusus and the son of Drusus the elder (Augustus' adopted son) and Antonia the younger, he was considered by his contemporaries to be an unlikely candidate for emperor, especially in view of the infirmity from which he suffered, so much so that his family kept him away from public life until the age of forty-seven, when he held the consulship along with his nephew Caligula. It was probably this infirmity and the low political esteem he enjoyed that enabled him to survive the purges that affected many members of the Roman nobility during the reigns of Tiberius and Caligula: when the latter died, Claudius became emperor precisely because he was the only adult male of the Julio-Glaudian dynasty.

Despite his lack of political experience, Tiberius Claudius Caesar Augustus Germanicus, this was the name adopted after his acclamation as emperor, demonstrated remarkable qualities: he was an able administrator, a great patron of public building, an expansionist in foreign policy (under his command came the conquest of Britain, the annexation of Thrace, and the reorganization of the provinces of Noricum and Rhaetia), and a tireless legislator, personally presiding over the courts and going so far as to promulgate twenty edicts in one day. However, his position was made unsafe by opposition from the nobility, which led Claudius to put many senators to death. Claudius also had to endure many misfortunes in his private life-one of which may have been the source of his assassination. Claudius' reputation among ancient historians was certainly not positive; on the contrary, among moderns many of his works were reevaluated.

Imperial family and succession

Emperor Claudius was born in *Lugdunum* (present-day Lyons) in Gaul on 10 B.C. during his third military campaign in Germany, under the name Tiberius Claudius Drusus, the third son of Nero Claudius Drusus (Elder Drusus) and Antonia Minor, after Germanicus and Livilla.

Claudius' father was the son of Tiberius Claudius Nero and Livia Drusilla, but he was born three months after Livia married Augustus; the emperor Tiberius was therefore Claudius' paternal uncle. Antonia Minor, on the other hand, was the daughter of the triumvir Marcus Antonius and Octavia Minor, sister of Augustus. In 4, following the adoption of his brother Gaius Julius Caesar Claudian Germanicus into the Julian family, Claudius became the *pater familias* of the *Claudii Nerones* and took the name Tiberius Claudius Nero Germanicus.

Conquest of Britain (43-51)

In 43 he began the conquest of Britain, almost a century after Gaius Julius Caesar. Beyond the political, economic, and military reasons for the expedition, one perhaps more important consideration, psychological in nature, should not be forgotten, and that is to prove to all that he was the worthy son of the conqueror of Germania, Drusus. He went to Britain in the autumn of the first year of the war to be present at the final victory. This was the conquest of which Claudius was most proud.

Parto-Armenian crisis (54)

The lands of the Kingdom of Armenia, between the Black Sea and the Caspian Sea, had long been a source of contention between Rome and the Parthian empire for control of the region. Nero, concerned that the Parthian king, Vologese I, had placed his own brother Tiridates on the throne of the Kingdom of Armenia in late 54, was convinced that it was necessary to initiate war preparations for an imminent military campaign, the command of which was eventually entrusted to Gnaeus Domitius Corbulonus. Under his command a pair of legions were also sent from the Danubian limes: the V *Macedonica* and the VIII *Augusta*. Also present in the eastern area were Legions X *Fretensis* and XII *Fulminata*, also celebrated in the coinage of the period (which may have sent their colonists to *Patrae*).

Nero

Last of the Julio-Claudian dynasty was Nero. Born as Lucius Domitius Enobarbus, he was the fifth and last emperor of the Julio-Claudian dynasty who, succeeding his uncle Claudius in the year 54, ruled for fourteen years until his suicide at the age of thirty. Initially, Nero left the government of Rome to his mother and his guardians, particularly Seneca. However, as he became an adult, his desire for power increased: he had his mother and guardians executed.

During his reign there was a series of revolts and rebellions throughout the Empire: in Britain, Armenia, Parthia, and Judea. Nero's inability to handle the rebellions and his substantial incompetence quickly became evident, and in 68 so that even the Praetorian Guard abandoned him. Nero committed suicide in 68, and after his death a new civil war broke out that ended the following year (in 69), known as the year of the four emperors, at the end of which Vespasian obtained the throne.

Imperial family

His father belonged to the Domizi Enobarbi family, a lineage considered to be of "plebeian nobility" (i.e., recent), while his mother, Agrippina Minor, was the daughter of the acclaimed leader Germanicus, granddaughter of Mark Antony, Agrippa, and Augustus, and sister of Emperor Caligula.

When in 41, her uncle Caligula was assassinated, Agrippina Minor returned to Rome from exile (as she was involved in a conspiracy against her brother Caligula), and a few years later (in 49), she managed to marry Emperor Claudius, obtaining his revocation of Seneca's exile, in order to use the famous philosopher as her son Nero's new tutor. At the age of eleven, Nero was forced by his mother to become engaged to Octavia, Claudius' eight-year-old daughter, thus becoming the rightful heir to his stepfather Claudius.

Military campaigns in Armenia (58-63)

Nero, concerned that the king of Parthia, Vologese I, had placed his own brother Tiridates on the throne of the kingdom of Armenia, decided to send one of his own valiant generals, Gnaeus Domitius Corbulonus, to head military operations in the East. The latter, once he had reorganized his army, penetrated Armenia in 58 and arrived as far as the capital Artaxata and succeeded in seizing it after beating Tiridates himself. The following year it was Tigranocerta's turn. At the end of the operations, in 60, he placed Tigrane V on the throne of Armenia.A new crisis broke out in 62, following which, the army of the governor of Cappadocia, Lucius Caesenius Peto, was beaten by Parthian-Armenian forces, Corbulone was forced to intervene. He in fact reached a final agreement with the "king of kings" in 63, restoring Rome's prestige, and concluding with Tiridates I of Armenia (who had replaced Tigrane V) an agreement that recognized the Roman protectorate and remained virtually unchanged until the principate of Trajan (98-117).

Celebrated Peace and closing of the Temple of Janus

Under Nero, the Parthian king Vologese I placed his own brother Tiridates on the throne of the kingdom of Armenia in late 54.This convinced Nero that it was necessary to initiate war preparations for an imminent military campaign.Domitius Corbulone was sent to quell the continuing skirmishes between the local populations and scattered groups of Romans. In reality there was no real war until 58 CE. After conquering Artaxata in 58 and the city of Tigranocerta in 59, he placed King Tigrane IV of the Parthians on the throne in 60. The new king was not very favorable to the influence of the Romans, and his brother Tiridates took his place in 64.

Thus the last outbreak of war was extinguished, and Nero was able to boast the title of *Imperator (Pacator)* by crowning King Tiridates I in Rome and inaugurating, at the same time, the celebrations of the three-hundredth anniversary of the first closing of the gates of the temple of Janus Geminus for the ecumenical peace achieved throughout the empire. Nero had a coin minted on which, on the obverse appears his figure with a crowned head and proud appearance bearing the inscription, " *IMP NERO CAESAR AVG GERM* " and on the reverse the temple of Janus "with closed doors" with the inscription, "*PACE P R UBIQ PARTAIANVM CLVSIT S C.*" Thus for the first time an emperor of Rome bore the title of Emperor.

Praetorian guard

Nero, seeing how Caligula had been killed and his adoptive father, Claudius, elected by the Praetorian Guard, decided to obtain his consent over the years, as is also evident from coins, especially from the last years of his reign.

Administrative and fiscal arrangements

Some of Nero's coins also celebrated some administrative and fiscal measures such as the frequent *congiaria in* addition to the annona for the supply of grain for the city of Rome.

Public Works

Emperor Claudius was the first to have a new port built about 4 km (or 2.5 miles) north of Ostia, known as *Portus*, on an area of about 70 hectares, equipped with two long piers jutting out over the Tyrrhenian Sea, with an artificial island and a lighthouse. The construction of this lighthouse was implemented by filling a large ship that had transported from Egypt a large obelisk used to decorate the Vatican circus. It was completed by his adopted son, Nero, who celebrated its completion with coinage. Nero gave the name *Portus Augusti* to the new port.

A triumphal arch was commissioned in honor of Emperor Nero, decreed by the Senate in 58, on the occasion of his victory over the Parthians, although it was not actually built until 62. It was located on the approach to the Capitol, but was probably destroyed shortly thereafter, either by *damnatio memoriae* or in the hill fire of 69. Depictions on coins show it with a single fornix, with free-standing Corinthian columns above pedestals projecting from the facade that supported statues and rich sculptural decoration.

In 64, under Nero's reign a frightful fire nearly razed the entire city, destroying three of the Augustan areas entirely and severely damaging seven, leaving only four intact. To encourage an orderly reconstruction and prevent the spread of new fires, a new city plan was enacted, implemented, however, only partially, as Tacitus reports, through the construction of wider streets, flanked by porticoes, with no common walls between buildings, of limited height, and with an almost banned use of flammable materials, replaced by stone and brick. Taking advantage of the destruction Nero built his *Domus Aurea*, which occupied the spaces between Caelian, Esquiline (Oppio) and Palatine with an enormous villa, a tangible sign of the emperor's autocratic aims. Other Neronian public buildings were the market on the Caelian (*Macellum Magnum*) and the Baths of Nero in the Campus Martius, whose regular and symmetrical plan served as a model for all future bath buildings, inaugurating the "imperial" typology of baths.

There is also speculation that the temple was rebuilt after the great fire of 64, at the same time as the house of the Vestal Virgins was moved and enlarged: in fact, the temple was depicted on coins from the time of Nero and subsequent Flavian emperors.

Other books by United Library

https://campsite.bio/unitedlibrary

Milton Keynes UK
Ingram Content Group UK Ltd.
UKHW051256220624
444380UK00018B/660